The Waterman's Children

The
Waterman's
Children

John Bensko

University of Massachusetts Press
Amherst

Printed in the United States of America
LC 93-32434
ISBN 0-87023-901-5 (cloth); 902-3 (pbk)
Designed by Milenda Nan Ok Lee
Set in Centaur by Keystone Typesetting, Inc.
Printed and bound by Thomson-Shore, Inc.

Library of Congress Cataloging-in-Publication Data
Bensko, John, 1949–
    The waterman's children / John Bensko.
        p.   cm.
    ISBN 0–87023–901–5 (alk. paper).—ISBN 0–87023–902–3 (pbk.:
alk. paper)
    I. Title.
PS3552.E547655W37   1994   93–32434
811'.54—dc20   CIP

British Library Cataloguing in Publication data are available.

For Patricia and John
my mother and father

Acknowledgments

Some of the poems in this manuscript appeared first in the following publications:

The Black Warrior Review: "My Mother, the Cause of It All" and "Mr. Trent's Memorabilia Room"

Chelsea: "In the Everglades" and "Away from It All"

Cincinnati Poetry Review: "The Craft of the Lame"

The Florida Review: "Virginia Beach"

The Gettysburg Review: "A Passing Blow"

The Iowa Review: "The Waterman's Children," "Escaping Eden," and "Crabbing"

Mississippi Review: "Why the Uncurious Travel" and "The Right Subject"

New Letters: "East Point, Bill's Grocery, and Love" and "The Cave Diver." Reprinted with permission of the curators of the University of Missouri.

New Orleans Review: "The Children of Goodwill"

The Panhandler: "The One Next Door"

Ploughshares: "After *A Day in the Country*" and "Growing up on the Lively Art of Painting"

Poetry: "The Wild Horses of Assateague Island," "My Wife's Desire," and "Imagery without Purpose"

Poetry Northwest: "Our Friend, the Photographer of Our Wedding" and "The Dancing Islands"

Shenandoah The Washington and Lee University Review: "A Guide to Trusting the Natives"

The Southern Review: "The Pet Store"

Contents

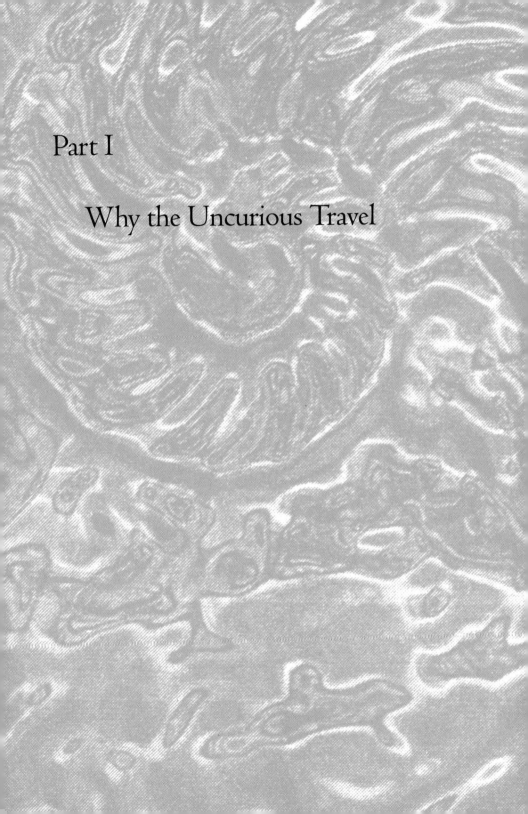

Part I

Why the Uncurious Travel

The Right Subject

—near Yauco, Puerto Rico

In the rain forest ahead
The road crossed a bridge,

The donkey standing
Alone in the middle

Wore a patchwork blanket
Of blue and red,

One front hoof dangled
From a few

Bloody ligaments.
We wanted to end it

Painlessly.
We thought of shooting him

Or running over him with the car.
There was nothing we could do.

As we stared off

Into the ravine

People drove by waving.
Down the mountainside

The stream broke
Into white torrents.

It was swallowed
Under lush green trees.

We left him,
Almost believing the right subject

Could still appear,
The rain forest was still

The perfect background,
We would make that picture.

East Point, Bill's Grocery, and Love

Becoming another person
is only a state away, you told me.
Again, again, again.
From the flat oppression of heat
down on head and shoulders
in the apartment lot,
day after day you spring the door
with names like Fred or Sammy
stitched red over the pockets
of workshirts you've found
strewn in the back cooler at Bill's.
The cooler is you, stripped
in its breakdown, turned
to a shelf for clothes.

Across the road men heave burlap . . .
sacks of oysters
if they crunch on the pier
and sacks of crabs if they rattle.
I am finding myself by what I can
and can't distinguish.
The cry of a gull
when it's hungry and when it's not.

The gulls come circling in.
What is marriage but finding

a new man each day in the bedroom
trying someone else's shirt?
The old grease, the old
names, never come out.
You are Bob, Bill, Harry
faster than I can tell,
faster than it took to move
from Virginia to Florida
to Tennessee and back. In the old jig

we hear at Bill's
in the afternoons when everyone
hangs along the drink machine,
you and I are working out
who you will be tomorrow
from the five shirts spread
on the checkerboard floor.
Step over here and look again.
Step over there.
In love enough
to look over my shoulder
from the gray hair
of a state on down the line,
I might call this
a dance one day.
Who can tell? Who can ever tell?

Why the Uncurious Travel

At the hotel, five rooms and a toilet
above a fabric shop, the owner
returns to my door, holding pliers.
No pliers . . . ice, I repeat.
His face changes to suggest
"ice" might mean I am leaving.
No . . . forget, I say waving him off.

On the pier a man eating an ice cream cone
simply lets it drop in the water.
A boy playing a harmonica wears a T-shirt
which has on the back: four footprints
walking in the direction of his head.
Flies are buzzing over an eel
which, dying, curled in the shape of an O.

The last person to speak correctly
informed me: *Simply beautiful down there.*
At the water's edge, the language
of two women shelling peas
tells me nothing but secrecy

and excitement. The sounds are not affected
by any need of mine to know.

When the boy's harmonica strays
to a tune suggesting sadness
and the glare off the ocean seems to soften
in the afternoon sun, it's quickly broken up
by a cab driver who squeals his tires
to the end of the pier. He opens his trunk
and begins to throw luggage into the water.

Escaping Eden

Maybe they don't want to remember
where exactly,
or maybe they can't
because everything
down miles of coastline
is very new,
or else it wears
the same abandoned face
of salt and sun bleached
neglect.

But somewhere
is where they stayed,
the tiny room
with the huge radio
receiving only one station
and the sink dripping
all night
while on the bed
they made
my beginning.

My mother remembers
the bus ride down from Tallahassee,
how a woman
passed out from heat

and they laid her in the aisle
where the curves
in a constant,
careless insistence
rocked her head
no.

My father remembers
a dock, which even then
was leaning
and the tide
draining the flats
until the view
was all of mud
and the low rough mounds
of oyster shells.
They watched the sunset
in misery.
The mosquitoes knew
as they did
it was too hot
to be inside.

Living north of here
I come along this road
and have to make up

my own place
of beginning.
I have gone against
their lack
of memory.
I have picked
an abandoned barracks
in the tall grass
under pines.

If there is a pier
it is hidden beyond the woods.
If there is a sunset
it comes here no longer
on the water
but through the trees.
I feel like the woman
on the bus
shaking my head
without knowing it,

not because I want
to unmake myself
but because
even if they could
tell me the truth,

it would be
here, among the scattered
bricks of an old
foundation post
and the rusty nails
lying in the sand
like petrified worms.

I can see
how the old pines
are twisted from a storm
and all are bent
away from the sea.
I can hear the insects
whose wings buzzing
are here the same
as they always have been
everywhere.

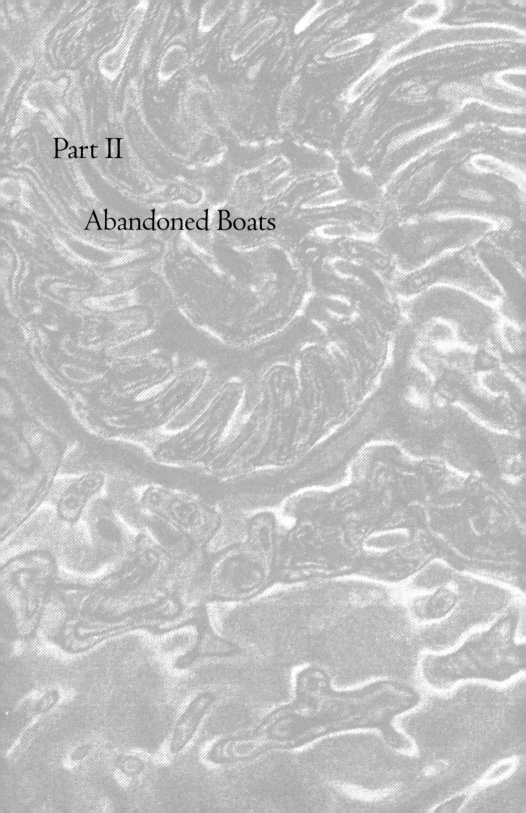

Part II

Abandoned Boats

Abandoned Boats

Who were the hands that brought you here?
Even the old when we were young
did not know. The rain had settled you.
The snails and slugs moved in.

Beyond the tideline you rode
the shore, buoyant, your rudders bent,
the thick wood scarred where oysters
were whacked clean. Your peeling hulls

pointed inland like needles
to treasure. Pirates, explorers,
we were stranded, lost.
We pulled the ropes to make you sail,

we scuffled your decks like crabs.
Down in the hold the gunnysacks
lay like the dead. Damp with oil and salt
they breathed but would not talk.

Imagery without Purpose

On the white wall of the porch
the lizard is motionless while the gray cat
flexes its claws and stretches
in a rectangle of sunlight.
Watching the lizard, the cat's eyes
seem to close, as if the effort
of the chase, though now at a standstill,
has become too much.
The scent of freshly cut pine
rises from the new boards
where rain rotted the steps.
With its perfume
the rampant cascade of honeysuckle
nearly encases the two rows
of hedge along the walk
to the front gate.

That taste? Metal filings . . .
the blades of the shovel
and the hoe were dull.
Filing them down to bright edges
somehow gets the taste
into the mouth,
a mixture of dirt and steel. Sweat,
trickling down the forehead as it runs
down strands of hair

and through the eyebrows, burns
as it hits the eyes.

How much do these images
accomplish? They will clear
the yard, until the smell
of freshly cut grass, the feel
of turned earth in the flower beds,
and the sight of new white
paint gives one cause
to retire to the porch swing
and wonder: *What should I feel?*
Not touch, smell, nor taste
of the honeysuckle,
but the need
for which all this has been prepared.

No one comes. And only the one
who waits, sipping the cool glass
of lemonade, will have expected her.

A Husband Floats Free

In the front yard
Up to his ears
In the watery
Life of a pirate
He lies in the kids'
Plastic pool and shouts
Skull and bones—Skull and bones
When neighbors jog by

He yells after them
Think of me
As an atmospheric
Depression
The industrious stop
Offering cash
To take our rusting Ford

His motto: love the hell
Out of spring
Give the lush
Weeds their way
Until they've shown you

The best work
Is none at all

The water laps
His legs and the sun
Warms his ears and arms
He looks peacefully
Out: the great green
Wave of kudzu
Is investing our house

Mr. Trent's Memorabilia Room

Pointing to walls covered with plastic-sealed
newspapers from the twenties,
my landlord tells me
of their *historical and sentimental value.*
I've come to pay the rent.

But once more I'm given the lesson:
To refuse to see the past is to refuse
to admit your failures.
He says his wife never missed a day
without reminding him of something bad.

I never know how to take his jokes.
They may or may not
tell me how bitter he is.
He grows nervous, then serious, and folds
his hands, a jovial but worried priest.

Turning his head a little sideways, as if

to get a new perspective,
he reachs into a drawer,
draws out a treasure
and asks me what I think.

I think. And I think
he's nuts. But I say, *how beautiful,*
and take the carving of a girl, the length
of my hand, her nude mahogany body
stretched along a wooden feather.

Where did she come from?
He laughs, shifting to the voice
of a drunkard: *Shoot! Don't ask me.*
There's only three things I know:
cigarettes, whiskey, and pocket knives.

Looking past him, I'm drawn to the window,
the one space in the room which says

nothing of the past. His wife.
The little woman, as he calls her.
The pale, rouged face looks out

from her 1930s oval portrait,
lips parted, as if about to speak.
Was it her? I ask, feeling the smooth wooden legs.
Yes. . . . He takes her from my hands.
The one time he has not

said less by saying more.
Leaving the rent on the table
I thank him for the tour.
His hands twist over the statue
like inefficient knives.

The One Next Door

We neighbors tell
how when her husband died
she dressed in white
and wrapped a white towel

around her head. She carries
on daily conversation
with him on the sidewalk.
She preaches:

*Welfare is a form of
prostitution.* For hours
each day she's in her yard,
sweeping the faded grass.

At parties when the fun
dies, we have little else:
our host, drunk, proposes
to pull down his trousers

and shock her back to *our*

way of thinking. Later,
the wives are wondering:
What if our husbands were

to die tomorrow? *She*
eats cats, a voice shouts
from the kitchen. As if that
might be the answer.

The Craft of the Lame

The lame can only go so far
before they turn into the thin
gold wire the craftsman has spun
to create the rigging of his ship.

It sits in my window, an expression
of his wish to be left alone.
When I went into his shop to buy it
he said: *The ship is not for sale.*

Because I live across the street
I have watched him all winter
coming slow like a man on crutches to work
and leaving after dark.

In the shop I watched the carrousel he'd made
as the blue and purple backs of the glass
horses turned from the touch of my hand.
How much for the ship? I said. He waved his finger.

The gesture must have meant: *anything . . .*
but anything will not be enough.
He has remained to me faceless,
almost undefined, except

as a heavy coat, a hat pulled low

over the head, a pair of illusory
crutches. Then the finger waved again, *yes, maybe.*
A voice said: *The ship is not for sale, but this . . .*

I remember the persistence with which I stayed
as he moved around the shop
leaning toward each inseparable piece
until I thought they would fall.

The Water Worker's Ghost

Not now so much in dreams, as in the afternoons
you think of me, my orange hat
and brown shirt like leaves in the yard.

Can I be simply a worker gone, like those
in the red ditch roadside of our house
whose knees, and waists, and shoulders dropped,

until all that was left were sunny hats
tilting and turning like toys on the ground?
Press your foot, feel the warmth

of their leavings from where the frost
had not hardened. The long strip of earth
is enough for a street of husbands

head to foot. We'll settle down
I told you. And I have. But you

are still moving. These afternoons of fall

set you to thinking. You're like the grass
will be in spring, not so much moving
to cover its scar, as to stretch itself out

where someone else has made a place. Maybe it's just
this spell of winter, but you're ready to go inside.
Turn on the water, let it run until clear.

Growing up on the Lively Art of Painting

The boat sailing over from the island dock,
about to capsize near the harbor buoy,
was a splash of red and white paint his father
knew would catch the boy's eye. *Action,*
unlike the fine detail of foaming lace
on the white-capped water: true action, his father
said, lives in the mystery of the half-seen.

The boy was speechless. The painting showed the day
he nearly drowned, tacking his dinghy across the sudden
gust from the approaching storm.
The same harbor was snugly painted, brown,
distant behind him. The buoy appeared
to swing its mad, bell-ringing confirmation
of the thunderheads springing from the low

dark sky. Reduced to that splash of red and white,
he wondered how his father standing with an easel
could have caught him there. Now, years later,
he still expects the distant observer,
paint in hand, that someone outside
who measures with his thumb and says,
action, action . . . while the unfelt springs on you

like beauty.

Below Sopchoppy, Florida

She has passed it
a hundred times,
the little shack surrounded
by swept dirt and the shade
of a tall, wide oak,
the sign at the door
saying always: Fresh Caught Today.

But now the tires
are spinning through
the sand ruts of the turnoff
and the engine has stopped
and in the moments after
she hears from within the house
a buzzing tune of comb and paper.

Climbing the steps, she sees
the thin child wavering
behind the screen door.
Between his blackened heel
and toes, the white arch
of his left foot curves about
the door, opening it slowly.

He says nothing,

nodding yes, shrugging no.
The sliver of ice
and the fish she buys
he hands her from the rusty chest
like a treasure of newsprint.
Its eyes are gone
from clear to fog.

In her house among the pans and pots
the evening light falls gray
as his face on the counter.
She unwraps his dirty feet,
his scraped knees. In a shack
with doors unlocked, she thinks,
your parents do not care

how I have taken you with me,
knife in hand, cutting the strips,
dipping them in batter.
They have come home from the shore
with their nets and cages
and caught no more of you

than the afternoon asleep

like the hound in the dirt
by your playthings.
Is it true? she asks.
Will even something from the bottom
of a watery chest
cook up crisp as I please?
He answers, and his voice creaks

in the shade of her kitchen
like an old tree in the wind.
You are alone.
But for now you have me.

The Dancing Islands

It began with the photo
of the patterned shade
of palm trees, covering
the model and her bikini
with the intricate fingers
of hallucination.
The brochure said:
*The French have a word
for it:* au pair,
*the quaint guest-house
where you'll spend the night.*

It ended with my look
back from the airstrip
to the small, postcard
town with its red tile roofs
and the fields
of cotton and sugar cane
against the green slopes
of the volcano,
changing shades
as the clouds
drifted over.

The plane had touched down

feathering an engine.
My bags had disappeared.
I had what I'd carried on:
a pint of gin
and eleven dollars.
There was no quaint term
for the guest-house
where I spent the night.

What they don't tell you is:
when you step into the shower
and find there the trickle
of water from the cistern
you simply cup your hands,
gather the water,
and splash it on your head.
Here is the trick:
the four-inch-long
black centipede
which lives between the stones
at the bottom of the shower

does not like the water.

Wonderful, your feet are islands.
Your fingers are palm trees.
The girl is your own
breathless anticipation.
Now you're learning. The brochure
has plans for anything:
Get away from it all.
Dance your heart away.

The Children of Goodwill

Their mothers work here
sorting clothes, taking turns at the register.
The children play with the phonographs.
They spin marbles on them
until each flies off. They gather
everything that turns and they turn them
all at once: a rusted fan, a globe
with a hole near Los Angeles
where a finger pushed through,
the wheels of three warped bicycles
balanced on their sides.

The feeling of surprise: like an old
love letter which changes each time
we read it, making us feel closer
or more distant, it depends on the movement
of all we've abandoned. The children
delight in keeping their worlds
in motion. We step through,
balancing on our way to the bookshelves
and they spin at our feet, laughing.

Happy in the junk
you and I and others have left out,

in the pieced-together rooms,
couches, chairs, and beds
on which we've given up,
they visit the world. *Surprise!*
They come at us shouting
and we're in the center
of a game we played when young:
spinning on our feet, until dizzy,
we don't know where we are.

A Guide to Trusting the Natives

Stuffing the menu

under his stained sleeve,
the waiter, who is also
the owner, tells us: *Fish is fish.*
You want to see?

Back of the kitchen
in a foot tub filled with ice
we find eels, red eyes
like fungus, and teeth

for a week of nightmares.

The cook loves to lean down,
smile through his dirty beard,
and say: *They all good.*
His son catches them.

Once your choice is cooked,
you may notice the similarity

to the delicate white flesh
that paralyzed the early explorers.

Beer is the only antidote.

Watch the clear green waters
across the bay. The boats
tipping their masts. As the sun
sets, you can eat here

for the rest of your life.

Part III

The Wild Horses
of Assateague Island

North Florida Bunker

Looking back from where
the nightwatch moon surrounds us
we think how desperate he was.

He lay in the dark, his back
warmed by the concrete. The air turned
cool on his face

and he knew the ammo stacked below
was sleeping men.
Bare in its fabric

of bobbing lights
from the off-course steamer,
love chilled him.

The sea oats, wave after wave,
saber the dunes.
Like us, he would call

his loneliness
the past. He would live where
his children roam

the rusting chambers to find

what they will.
Not war,

gentle feelings
make our world
impossible to protect.

Meanwhile, he defended nothing
against nothing.
His body blew

so slowly through the salt air
his blood vanished
before it reached the walls.

Here as lovers
scrawling our names
we remember him.

We make ourselves
a future we can feel.
We guard the interior

of our forgetfulness.

The Cave Diver

Dear, the light goes out.
The last sight of the shelf
of white crystal
flowing in front of me
in its permanent waterfall
hangs in the darkness,
then fades.

Like a crawl space
through water and rock
my last days with you
have tightened my fingers
to claws. They pull me through
room after room.

If my eyes are open
I don't know.
My silly breath bubbles
from the mouthpiece.
The clang of air
strapped to my shoulders
tries to sound like hope.

As much as air
I need the silence
to match

your darkness.
I hear confusing
echoes. I claw my way

on, the silted rock
sliding through my fingers.
I draw you past me
like the world.
Its knobs and crevices,
the leavings of your voice
bump me along.

Away from It All

No two are alike
In the handful of tiny shells
My husband scoops from the tideline
Along the beach.

By now our boy,
Old enough to go alone and play,
Shows no interest in his father's
New discoveries.

He walks away
Dragging his tattered kite
Like the remains of a Christmas tree.
Be back, he says.

Nothing sums up
The way I feel about them. The cool surf
Sucks down my feet in the sand.
The sun cracks my skin.

Vacations crowd us

Into restaurants, onto beaches.
All that loneliness spills
To somewhere else.

Small crabs. Sand
Dollars. Periwinkles digging in.
He likes to stop where something strange
Is happening.

If I had my way
I would keep on driving, towns
Breezing past the windows like
Unanswered friendships.

Always we keep
Coming back, so neither is satisfied,
And now they know us, expect us
The same weekend.

I will give up.
Will leave out the happiness

Of nearly falling from the pier when the fish
Sings out my line.

Instead I will go
To him, say that I love him, and bend down
Over him as he forms the shells into
Fortresses.

In India
People are starving. So the story
Goes, finding the weakness
In us all.

My Wife's Desire

Talking of the looks
of excessive joy and sorrow
in the African masks,
she stops to watch the line
of people wandering
between the pedestals
of the museum sculptures.
Slow, oddly quiet,
they let their fingers stray
across the stone, the bronze.
Noticing their uniformed guides,
she understands they are blind.

She is jealous, unsatisfied.
To look is enough. But to see
those others taking part
in something beyond her
both sad and rewarding
changes her. She wants to pretend
she is one of them.
It's worth the possibility
of being found out.
In dark glasses, she follows them.

The way she is posing,
stumbling forward

with her hands held out,
I'd feel absurd. But once
after we made love in the dark
she explained: it was the way to put off
the embarrassment of her body.
With her eyes closed, the disembodiment
completes her.
Her fingers are absolved
taking in the stone, the bronze
beyond exaggeration.

Crabbing

Who was I
but a shuffling sideways
who weaved whatever path
the current took as it swirled
from the pilings out?
Reaching the backbone
and the string
that held it hanging
my pull was no more
than a little wind,
there and then not there.

And who were you
as gentle as I,
slow like the current,
hand over hand
drawing me in,
depending
on what you could not see?
We became
the wavering shadows.

While across the river
the sawgrass marshland

stretched to the ocean.
The spindly heron
like a gray exclamation
of patience
had been standing one-legged
for an hour.
The afternoon heat
lay on the dock
in the faint, sweet smell
of pitch released.

Posey's

Knowing that to the north
the tide invades
my thin road home

and that the pull
of the steamy afternoon
will keep me here afloat

he leans a tad more,
curving like a chameleon
against the out-of-kilter wall.

He says I fit right in.
Like the window beside us
I've lost my sense

of direction,
a frame of pieces
going their own way.

Behind the bar
his black gloved hands
begin to shuck the oysters.

A twist of the rounded knife
cracks them

like huge gray knuckles.

He is swift and sure. He flicks
the worthless halves
into a bucket by my knees.

He lays the others before me.
Time after time, not knowing
why, I have watched him lean

while the hunch
of his shoulders points him
south, to the river, the marsh,

in any case, the back room.
Or is he the same one
as last time? He seems

different, the brother
or cousin of the last one,
like a curving

channel through sawgrass
or a strange, dismal love
which may or may not return.

After *A Day In The Country*

—on the film by Jean Renoir

My wife says they might be Laurel
and Hardy: the thin, future
son-in-law, Anatole, and the fat
father of his Henriette, who clown
with fishing poles at the river's
edge. *Pike!* the fat one says.
And the thin one—*Did you say:*
the shark that lives in fresh water?
Cuts bone like bread, the fat one says.

Meanwhile, the mother and daughter
seduced by the country gentlemen
tumble in the grass. True *Parisienne,*
the mother plays the satyr's prize.
In a grove by the river
the daughter, ruined, is once
and for all in love. *I will never*
forget you, her young man says.
And she returns—*Will you? Will you?*

We pick them up years later.
Henriette returns to the country,
meets her lover, and cries. The last image
of her rowing off in the boat
while Anatole, now her husband,
fumbles in the stern

with his fishing pole
is meant to tell us something
about life, about love.

The audience won't buy it.
Is that all? they say.
Where the artist's impression
of rain falling on the river
ends, our romance, the one liner,
begins. *I will never forget you,*

I whisper. And my wife returns—
Will you? Will you? You pike, you shark
of fresh water!

Virginia Beach

Beneath the sky
you said was white grapes
clustered against a blue
tablecloth, you watched

the young girl, barely
in her teens, smile,
turn somersaults,
and let her beautiful

green eyes wander
the length of my body.
Eight months pregnant,
you told me how

unnatural you were,
and I laughed. You felt
like the sunken car
behind us in the dunes.

The girl stood on her head.
Her thin, brown legs

moved with a freedom
which overcame

your jealousy.
You said you should be home
forgetting yourself.
Even so, like the long, bending

necks of the sea oats,
you were rising above me.

Our Friend, the Photographer of Our Wedding

At the reception he photographed shoes,
hands on the punchbowl, and coats
piled on the bed. Because he learned
in school what's new is necessary,
all family portraits are fisheyed.

He said: *These are not ordinary*
pictures. You get a chance like this
once in a lifetime. At the ceremony
he got us wide angle with our heads
cut off. The justice of the peace,

who turned out to be a judge
standing on a sheepskin rug
to renew his feet, said the words.
The flash went. We kissed.
Later we found a largemouth bass

gliding from its mount on the wall
over the tops of our heads had attracted
the shot. In the family fishbowl
my wife in the bulging center already
looked pregnant. *What realism,* he said.

He pointed to the shrunken figures

blurred off at the edges. *Grandparents.*
If only we could have found the way
to thank him. For that series
of the honeymoon, especially,

a hundred shots of venetian blinds,
around-the-clock on a wall-sized poster.

The Wild Horses of Assateague Island

Although the sign says
Do not feed the horses,

my husband cannot help admiring
their docile looks, the delicate size

of their bodies, and the ease
with which they nibble

the crackers from his hands.
He says: *Why waste stale crackers*

when the least we can do
is make friends?

They lean across the picnic table
and stretch their lips.

Losing its fear, a small herd
drifts across the road toward us.

From behind the dunes

a string of ten or twelve

breaks into a run.
The car, he says, *run for it!*

The home movie later shows
tongues licking the windows,

lips and teeth caressing
the hood. My husband's mouth opens.

He is saying: *Sign? What sign?*
Under the perspective

of wild brown eyes peering in.

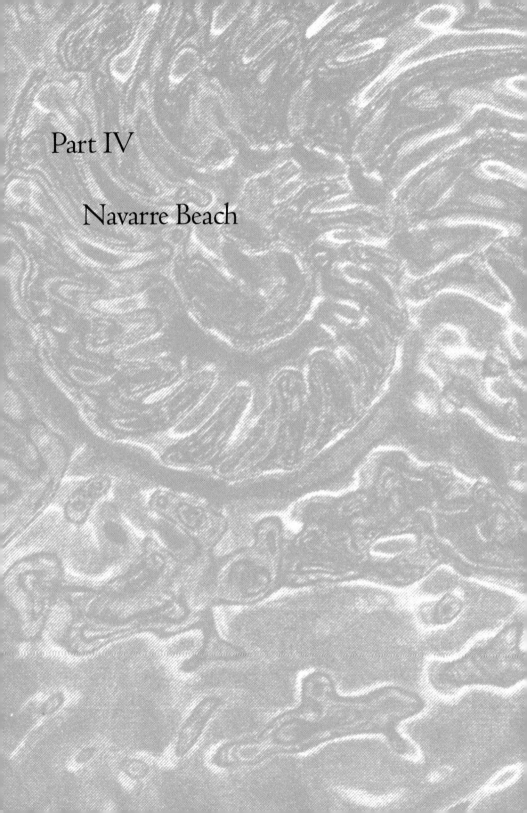

Part IV

Navarre Beach

Father Fear

While you stoop over the tidal slough
and tap your fingers in a trumpet riff
like the shuddering
of a wounded fish,

from my far weedy bank I launch
the two bumps of my eyes
and the twisting rough
snake of my tail.

Your daughter turns gray
as a stranded fish.
Your boy waves his arms, lost
as a balancing pelican.

Calm them as you will
with the prince and princess
of bedtime, I am a breath
beyond you on the verge

of moss oak and cedar swamp
with the tiny scree of the tree frog,
its green round toes sucking

the bark outside the window.

So let me glide
to the wounded. Let me
swirl and suck them down
in my long snapping mouth.

Let's get together on the truth.
Tell it! Life, my children,
is disconnected. I swim
in the shallows

of your sleep.
You come into my room.
Your tiny arms are shaking.
I rescue them.

Bull Minnows

A year ago we edged
the rippling shallows
of the tidal flats, toes barely in.

I saw too late
your wide eyes widening.
I knew how it was

to be smaller than them.
Now, the reed-lined pool shrinks
to its smallest inhabitants.

Young crabs joust our toes, then scurry.
The thumb-thick water snake
finds its home too shallow and, like

the black crest of a wave
taking the drained pond
as beneath it, slips through the grass

to open water. Time to wade
for minnows with my four-foot
cast net, while you skirt the pond

to herd them in. You are

as calm as the shadow you cast.
Your feet in the shallows,

you glide them across
the slippery mud. I think I know
how it is.

You come on the water
and drive them beyond you, inch long,
darting forward, helpless.

The Pet Store

Standing outside
late from school
I leaned to the cage of birds,
the bars shining in the sunlight
and the green and yellow bodies
flitting perch to perch,
with no sound coming
through the glass.

Could they see me?
I stubbed my finger on the pane.
They jumped and fluttered.
But they were always
fluttering, their round
black eyes wide
without expression,
the gray claws tight
around the bars.
Some were acrobats.
They hung upside down,
their wings flapping
to lift the cage
and push it to the ceiling.

Others, with their
curved, hard beaks

locked to the wire
twisted their necks
and swung.
They were on a ship
keeping their balance
while the deck
rocked wild.

I had heard they live
a few years, less
than I had been alive.
Not much time, I said,
watching the ones
who stood on the bottom.
They stroked their beaks
across their feathers.
They were calm as my mother
brushing her hair,
never hearing what I said
as I looked down
into that quiet,
just then finding
itself inside me.

In the Everglades

Where the wooden walkway came
from the tall grass
to a clear shallow pond,
my wife and I leaned
over the rail
and became shadows
with the shadows in the water:
the dim, green-lit figures
of the gar, the alligator,
and the diving cormorant.
We pointed to where

the world goes
past the herons perched
on limbs, to the soaring
indistinguishable wings,
to the clouds
like white nets
on the water.
Three years old that month
our son began to want
to take everything home.
He reached and tried
to name them: *bird . . . fish.*

The long, brown bodies

of two gar broke the surface.
Then they were back
lining themselves
with our shadows.
Bird, he said reaching.
He's being stubborn, my wife said.
To me, he was having fun . . .

the first delight of keeping
like the water
everything
stubbornly in place.

A Passing Blow

A child, I heard
the thump of his boots
on the boat's bottom.
He was cursing
at the snagged net.
I had no fear of his drowning
although I dreamed it many times.

First, the slip over the edge.
His feet rose. The cap
fell from his head.
His black hair thickened
like tar hitting the water.
His arms went under
heavy as logs.

He sank and sank.
But he had no need
of breathing. Air
would only hold him up.
At last at the bottom

landing like a cat
he walked to shore.

Tonight I float with him
in the overheated room.
The nurse bobs around.
My children chatter
and scud across the rug.
Unable to sink he breathes
the hours drowning.

Outside, the dried leaves
of the palm trees rattle.
The barbed wire creaks
where the loose post sways.
The edge of weather.
In his weak, dry voice
he talks of it, of how

the water in the bay
will not lap the pilings

or crash against them now
so much as heave itself past
in long, low swells.
Weather, coming onshore
a hundred miles away,

to wash the precarious roads,
to fling off the tin
whose last hold
on the rafters
was a few rusty nails.

The Old Map Marked "Phosphorescence Bay"

When the road we were on
met the road
we thought we were on
the drunk doing push-ups
on the bench outside
the lonely cantina
gave incoherent directions
in two languages.

To my mother, stationed
an hour away in World War II,
we were headed for the place
all the young officers
were asking her to. All
except my father.

Near midnight the road
was suddenly water.
I looked up from reading
Captain Marvel by flashlight

in time to see the waves lapping
the gravel at the pavement's edge.
Is this it? I asked.
Is this the bay?

. . . an open stretch
of water in the marshlands
we'd been skirting
for an hour.

My mother talked of boats
leaving hourly
from the hotel dock to drift
on the moonless water.
Below, pale green lights
swept the trails of things
she could not see.

As we turned the car

we found, as in the fairy tale,
what we *came* to see:
a collapsed hotel and a sign
in the faded
extravagance of signs:
See the cold embers of darkness
struck to brilliance.

Striped tropical frogs
the size of small rabbits
leaped before the headlights.
There was the buzz
of gnats and mosquitoes,
the deep occasional
thunk of a frog.

No, my mother said. *No.*
And my father smiled.

Dr. Kirk

White hair,·
thin body, notepad in her lap,
weekend upon weekend I took
the clay, slapped it flat, thumbed it up
on the board before her.
A field of red animals, an angel

whose wings were rivers.
And my parents in the hall,
waiting to carry me
the hundred miles home:
they rode in the car like clay,
never asking what happened,

molded in some trust
among adults that even children
can be solved.
So that, today I'm a patient third,
watching as though outside
a window, while inside

castles rise and rivers sprout bodies
I don't understand.
Her silence pushes me. Her hands,
though I can't see them,

must hold a pencil or a pen,
the words, hers alone,

still sinking into the page.
I am what I left her.
I'm a god
caught soundlessly
on a page, within the waiting
as she waits, an old woman, who watches,

writes in a book . . . an old woman
with no idea who I am,
who goes on writing me down
year after year in a hand
no one knows the way to read.
Until I am an angel whose wings are rivers,

and my child's body, its dozen animals,
is pressed into her.

The Terrorist

I am the unwanted child
You wish had stopped
Somewhere far from you,
Another country, another time.

You raised me anyway,
Imagining I was
Still back there, changing
My birth like a black mask.

You recognized me
Suddenly, again and again.
At the bank, the bus stop,
My bland face
Canceled your future.

Then I grew
Past the years of being new.
You read of me in the newspapers.
I was nothing

But print. You watched the television
And I flickered

On your floors
And on your walls.

Keeping me at such
A distance was all
You could do.
Then, I came home.

To let you know
I was wanted for more,
I was different than you
Had made me,

I stepped beyond
The shattered door,
The exploded glass
You had imagined.

My Mother, the Cause of It All

With my father
one thing must rightly follow

another. To foretell the ruin
of the family's trip to the Rockies

he said we'd catch the spotted fever.
But my mother claimed to have felt the symptoms

begin the night before.
He read to us how a doctor of national note

found travel by car will derange
the senses. She answered with her dream

of strange nuances in the tires. The car
held a mad whisper: *strange . . . insane . . . you are.*

No matter how hard he tried to predict things
into falling on us, she went before him,

fulfilling his horror.
Why should the right follow the wrong?

Before we left Fort Worth, he was describing

a breakdown in the desert: death

in ten miles . . . *no laughing matter.*
She began to pant: *a breakdown,*

I'm having a breakdown!
Our laughter defeated him. As voice of doom

he never existed. The mesas, the mountains
in the distance, the desert with its curtains

of dust blowing helter-skelter. Only the wide
open spaces are the cause

for the wide open spaces.
Without cause, he could not stop us.

The Waterman's Children

We hear his feet in thick boots
clattering the shells
as he drags the soggy nets
over the stern of the boat,
and the pinebark whisper of his breath
as he hangs the lines
from one tree to another.

We watch his face
coming onto the porch
like something from the sun,
deep red, so deep it is brown,
wrinkle on wrinkle,
turning to the father
we know, the eyes
lost among tight waves.

We feel his hands, so scarred
they're the shells of oysters.
Cut skin of the knuckles,
he comes at night and touches
our foreheads with his palm.
The inside we feel
has no pearl to disturb us.

Navarre Beach, December 1988

This is winter, the deserted locked pier, and the waves
at the end which are building. The sun as it sets
in a purple cloud dish to our right

seems to give consent to our climbing the fence,
no one near, to walk out in the dusk without fear
of arrest. Eight years old now, you were not

even born the last time I came here, in summer,
your mother in the dark motel room, even then
I suspect, knowing it would not work between us.

That warm day all the others and I stood here
casting lines without luck until late when it came:
the white log floating in, the drowned man

we followed down the pier as he rose, fell, drifted
back, then washed up the beach. Neither I nor anyone
could tell then what he had done to us.

The wind whipping your small green jacket, your blond hair,
makes you turn toward me. I cannot tell you why

your mother has left us . . . us, although

I can see it is not you but me she has left.
In winter the ocean darkens and turns heavy,
more lonely, but more powerful, huge

swells breaking through the pilings of the pier,
like a weakness gathered by the wind.